NEW HORIZONS IN
ENGLISH 1
SECOND EDITION

LARS MELLGREN
MICHAEL WALKER

Consulting Editor:
JOHN A. UPSHUR
English Language Institute
University of Michigan

▲ ADDISON-WESLEY PUBLISHING COMPANY
Reading, Massachusetts · Menlo Park, California · Don Mills, Ontario
Amsterdam · London · Manila · Singapore · Sydney · Tokyo

SOVANN

Illustrations by Akihito Shirakawa

Photographs: p. 63, courtesy of Judith Bittinger;
            p. 83, courtesy of Rafael Millán

Copyright© 1980, 1978, 1973 by **Addison-Wesley Publishing Company, Inc.**
Philippines copyright 1980, 1978, 1973. This work is based on *This Way* ©
Lars Mellgren and Michael Walker. All rights reserved. No part of this publi-
cation may be reproduced, stored in a retrieval system, or transmitted in any
form or by any means, electronic, mechanical, photocopying, recording, or
otherwise, without the prior written permission of the publisher. Printed in the
United States of America.

ISBN: 0-201-05010-2

    JKLM-WC-89876543

What's her name?	Mary	Her name is Mary.

1. What's her name?    Lucy   Her name is Lucy.

2. What's her name?   Carmen    Her name is Carmen.

3. What's her name?   Sally   Her name is Sally.

What's his name?	Ben	His name is Ben.

1. What's his name?   Mike   His name is Mike.

2. What's his name?   Don   His name is Don.

3. What's his name?   Peter   His name is Peter.

1. What's his name?   **Ben**   His name is Ben.

2. What's her name?   **Lucy**   Her name is Lucy.

3. What's her name?   **Mary**   Her name is Mary.

4. What's his name?   **Peter**   His name is Peter.

5. What's her name?   **Carmen**   Her name is Carmen.

6. What's his name?   **Mike**   His name is Mike.

7. What's her name?   **Sally**   Her name is Sally.

8. What's his name?   **Don**   His name is Don.

—Good morning, Tom.
—Good morning, Mary. Is his name John?
—No, it isn't.
—Well, what *is* it?
—It's Fred.

1.
—Is his name Ben?
—Yes, it is.

5.
—Is her name Lucy?
—Yes, it is.

2.
—Is his name John?
—No, it isn't.

6.
—Is her name Susan?
—No, it isn't.

3.
—Is his name Peter?
—No, it isn't.
—Well, what *is* it?
—It's Mike.

7.
—Is her name Carmen?
—No, it isn't.
—Well, what *is* it?
—It's Sally.

4.
—Is his name Don?
—No, it isn't.
—Well, what *is* it?
—It's Jack.

8.
—Is her name Mary?
—No, it isn't.
—Well, what *is* it?
—It's Carmen.

LISTEN & UNDERSTAND

BASICS

STATEMENTS:	His name is Tom. It's Tom.
SHORT ANSWERS:	Yes, it is. No, it isn't.
YES-NO QUESTION:	Is his name Tom?
INFORMATION QUESTIONS:	What's his name? What is it?

CONTRACTIONS:

what is ⟶ what's

it is ⟶ it's

is not ⟶ isn't

POSSESSIVE ADJECTIVES:

This is **my** **your** **his** **her** friend.

VOCABULARY/EXPRESSIONS

friend	Bye.
her	Glad to meet you.
his	Good-bye.
is	Good morning.
it	Hello.
my	Hi.
name	Pleased to meet you.
no	See you later.
this	So long.
what	Well...
yes	
you	
your	

What's this?		It's a hat.

hat	scarf	shirt	tie	jacket	raincoat

sweater	blouse	skirt	belt	dress	bathrobe

1. Is this a hat?   No, it isn't.

2. Is this a sweater?   Yes, it is.

3. Is this a blouse?   Yes, it is.

4. Is this a tie?   No, it isn't.

5. Is this a shirt?   Yes, it is.

6. Is this a dress?   Yes, it is.

| What's your favorite color? | It's blue. |

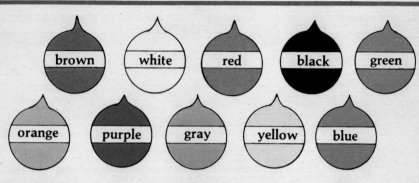

brown white red black green

orange purple gray yellow blue

1. What color is his shirt?

It's white.

2. What color is her hat?

It's gray.

3. What color is his suit?

It's black.

4. What color is his bathrobe?

It's orange.

5. What color is her skirt?

It's green.

6. What color is his jacket?

It's yellow.

What color are his shoes?		They're brown.

1. What color are his slacks? They're green.

2. What color are his shorts? They're white.

3. What color are his socks?  They're blue.

4. What color are her boots?  They're black.

5. What color are her slippers?  They're yellow.

6. What color are her jeans?  They're red.

7. What color are her glasses? They're orange.

What's he wearing?  He's wearing
a brown tie.

1. What's he wearing?  He's wearing
a green shirt.

2. What's she wearing? He's wearing
a red blouse.

3. What's she wearing?  She's wearing
a yellow sweater.

What's s(he) wearing?

What's he wearing? He's wearing white shorts.

1. What's she wearing? She's wearing green socks.

2. What's he wearing?  He's wearing black boots.

3. What's she wearing? She's wearing blue slacks.

What's s(he) wearing?

Joe is wearing a blue hat.

Sally is wearing a black sweater.

Koko is wearing yellow shoes.

Mike is wearing red slacks.

1. Who's wearing a blue hat?   Joe is.

2. Who's wearing a black sweater?   Sally is.

3. Who's wearing yellow shoes?   Koko is.

4. Who's wearing red slacks?   Mike is.

---

1. Is Mike wearing a red hat?   No, he isn't.

2. Is Mike wearing red slacks?   Yes, he is.

3. Is Sally wearing a red sweater?   No, she isn't.

4. Is Sally wearing a black sweater?   Yes, she is.

5. Is Mike wearing a red hat,
   or red slacks?   He's wearing red slacks.

6. Is Koko wearing a yellow blouse,
   or yellow shoes?   She's wearing yellow shoes.

7. Is Joe wearing a blue hat,
   or a blue tie?   He's wearing a blue hat.

8. Is Sally wearing a black sweater
   or a black skirt?   She's wearing a a black sweater.

PRONUNCIATION

I. Hello.
   Hello, what's your name?
   My name is Ben. What's *your* name?
   It's Sally.

II. Is your name Carmen?
    Is his name Peter?
    Is her name Sally or Lucy?
    Is she wearing a dress or a bathrobe?

III. Is your name Mike?
     No, it isn't. It's Tom.

     Who's wearing a red hat?
     Koko is.
     Who's wearing shorts?
     Peter is.
     What color are his shorts?
     They're white.

IV. Is he wearing a green tie, or a brown tie?
    He's wearing a green tie.

    Is she wearing shoes or boots?
    She's wearing boots.

    Is this your jacket?
    No, *that's* my jacket.

STATEMENT: Joe is wearing a blue hat.

CHOICE QUESTION: Is he wearing a blue hat,
or a red hat?

INFORMATION QUESTIONS: What's he wearing?
Who's wearing shorts?
What color is his tie?
What color are his shoes?
What's this?

ADJECTIVES:

Bill is wearing a
red
white shirt.
green

Judy is wearing
brown
black boots.
orange

TO BE FORMS:

What color **is** his hat?   His hat **is** brown.
What color **are** his shorts?   They **are** white.

DEMONSTRATIVE PRONOUNS:

This is her hat.   **That** is his hat.

BASICS

PRONOUNS:

Ben
Don ———→ he
Tom

Carmen
Lucy ———→ she
Mary

hat
sweater ———→ it
bathrobe

shorts
glasses ———→ they
shoes

CONTRACTIONS:

that is ———→ that's

who is ———→ who's

he is ———→ he's

she is ———→ she's

they are ———→ they're

VOCABULARY/EXPRESSIONS

a	glasses	scarf *foulard*	they
are	gray	she	tie
bathrobe	green	shirt	wearing
belt	hat(s)	shoes	white
black	he	shorts *coulotte*	who
blouse	jacket	skirt	yellow
blue	jeans	slacks *Pantalon*	
boots	or	slippers	Excuse me.
brown	orange	socks	Oh no it isn't.
color	purple	suit	Oh, Sorry!
dress	raincoat	sweater *chandaille*	
favorite	red	that	

TEST YOURSELF

I. 1. Hello, Lucy.
This is my friend Tom.

    a) Good morning.
    b) Glad to meet you.
    c) See you later.

2. See you later.

    a) Good morning.
    b) Yes, it is.
    c) Good-bye.

3. What's
    a) his
    b) her name?
    c) your

My name is Mary.

4. Is
    a) his
    b) her name Jack?

Well, what is it?

No, it isn't.
    a) It's Tom.
    b) What's Tom?
    c) This is my friend.

5. What's Bill wearing?

    a) He's
    b) She's wearing a jacket.
    c) It's

6. What color is
her blouse?

It's
    a) red.
    b) yellow.
    c) white.

7. What color is
his bathrobe?

It's
    a) orange.
    b) green.
    c) blue.

8. What color are
her shoes?

They're
    a) black.
    b) brown.
    c) purple.

9. What color are
his slacks?

    a) It's
    b) He's green.
    c) They're

II.

1. What's Sue wearing?   2. What's Bob wearing?

1. a hat
2. a sweater
3. socks
4. a blouse
5. a shirt
6. a skirt
7. a tie
8. a jacket
9. shoes
10. boots
11. a raincoat
12. shorts
13. glasses
14. slacks
15. slippers

III.

1. What's her name?   . . . .

2. . . . . ?   His name is Tom.

3. . . . . Peter?   No, it isn't.

4. What's this?   . . . . a green shirt.

5. Is this your hat?   No, ... My hat is green.

6. . . . . wearing a   Don is.
   red sweater?

7. . . . . a red raincoat?   Yes, she is.

Where's my jacket?

It's on the sofa.

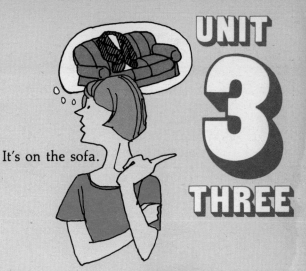

Where's my raincoat?

It's in the bedroom.

Where are my boots?

They're under the chair.

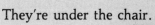

Where's the tie?
It's on the table.

Where's the hat?
It's on the chair.

Where's the belt?
It's under the chair.

Where's the shirt?
It's under the table.

1. Where's the raincoat? It's on the chair.

2. Where's the bathrobe? It's under the table.

3. Where's the scarf?  It's on the bed.

4. Where's the sweater?  It's under the sofa.

Lucy is in her bedroom.
Her hat is on the chair.
Her blouse is on the table.
Her scarf is on the floor.
Her bathrobe is on the bed.
Her slippers are on the rug.

1. Where's her hat?   It's on the chair.
2. Where's her blouse?   It's on the table.
3. Where's her scarf?   It's on the floor.
4. Where's her bathrobe?   It's on the bed.
5. Where are her slippers? They're on the rug.

Ben is in the living room.
His shirt is on the sofa.
His tie is on the chair.
His belt is on the table.
His socks are on the lamp.
His shoes are on the rug.

1. What's on the sofa?
2. What's on the chair?
3. What's on the table?
4. What are on the lamp?
5. What are on the rug?

What time is it?

2. It's two o'clock.

1. It's one o'clock.

3. It's three o'clock.

4. It's quarter to four.

5. It's quarter to five.

6. It's quarter past six.

7. It's quarter past seven.

8. It's half past eight.

9. It's half past nine.

10. It's ten-thirty.

11. It's eleven-thirty.

12. It's twelve o'clock. It's noon.

13. It's twelve o'clock. It's midnight.

What time is it now?

1.

2.

3.

AT THE BUS STOP

—Excuse me, what time is it?
—It's one o'clock.
—When is the next bus?
—I'm sorry, I don't know.

1. **2.**

—Excuse me, what time is it?
—It's half past one.
—When is the next bus?
—I'm sorry, I don't know.

3.

—Excuse me, what time is it?
—It's quarter to two.
—When is the next bus?
—I'm sorry, I don't know.

4.

5.

Mr. Jones Mrs. Rivera Mr. King Miss Black

Mr. Jones is in front of Mrs. Rivera.
Mrs. Rivera is in front of Mr. King.
Mr. King is in front of Miss Black.

Miss Black Mr. King Mrs. Rivera Mr. Jones

Mrs. Rivera is behind Mr. Jones.
Mr. King is behind Mrs. Rivera.
Miss Black is behind Mr. King.

Tom		Mary.
Mary	in front of	Bill.
Joe		Sally.
	is	
Lucy		Jack.
Peter	behind	Lucy.
Carmen		Peter.

| Where's | Tom? Joe? Peter? | He's | in front of... |
| Where's | Mary? Lucy? Carmen? | She's | behind... |

LISTEN & UNDERSTAND

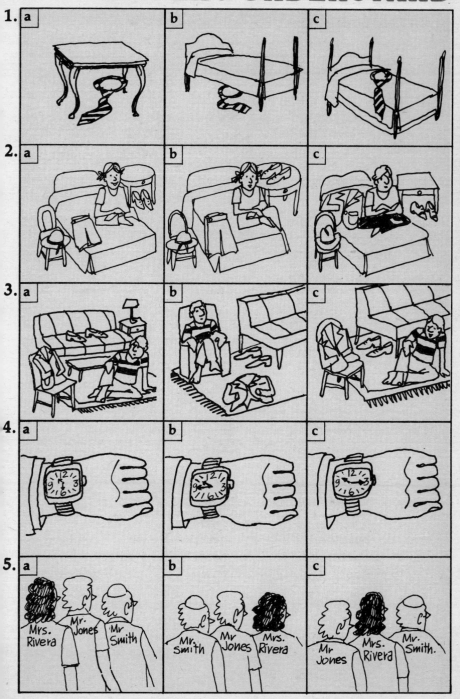

BASICS

DEFINITE ARTICLE THE:

> **The** tie is on **the** table.
>
> Don is in **the** living room.

INFORMATION QUESTIONS:

Where's the tie?	**What time** is it?
Where are the shoes?	**When** is the next bus?

CONTRACTIONS:

where is⟶where's	I am⟶I'm
do not⟶don't	

PREPOSITIONS:

The tie	**on**	
	under	the chair.
Mr. Jones	**in front of**	Mrs. Rivera.
	is **behind**	
Don		
	at	the bus stop.
Lucy	**in**	her bedroom.

VOCABULARY/EXPRESSIONS

at	in	on
bed	in front of	rug
bedroom	lamp	sofa
behind	living room	table
bus	midnight	the
bus stop	next	under
chair	noon	when
floor	now	where

What time is it?   two o'clock
                                quarter to ten
I'm sorry, I don't know.   quarter past six
                                half past five (five-thirty)

numbers one - twelve

—Who's that boy?
—Who?
—The boy in the green pants.
—Oh, that's Joe.

—Who's that girl?
—Who?
—The girl in the blue dress.
—Oh, that's Jane.

1. Who's this?   Lucy
   How old is she?
   What color is her hair?
   Is she thin or chubby?
   And what color are her eyes?

It's Lucy.
She's nineteen.
It's black.
She's chubby.
They're black.

2. Who's this?
   How old is he?
   What color is his hair?
   Is he tall or short?   Daniel
   And what color are his eyes?

It's Daniel.
He's thirteen.
It's blond.
He's short.
They're green.

3. Who's this?   Bill
   How old is **he**?
   What color is **his** hair?
   What color are **his** eyes?
   Is **he** thin or chubby?
   Is he tall or short?

It's **Bill**.
He's fourteen.
It's **red.**
They're **blue.**
He's chubby.
He's tall.

Elena

Joe

—Look at that **woman** over there.
—Where?
—There—the **woman**
  in the red dress.
—Oh, that's **Elena**.
—What's **her** last name?
—It's **Rivera**.

1. man/Sam/Chin

2. boy/Tim/Novak

—Look, this is Ted.
—Is he your new boyfriend?
—Yes, he is.
—What's he like?
—Well, he's thin. His hair is red,
  and his eyes are green. He's
  very tall and handsome. And
  he's seventeen.

—Look, this is Rita.
—Is she your new girl friend?
—Yes, she is.
—What's she like?
—Well, she's short and chubby.
  Her hair is blonde, and her
  eyes are blue. She's fifteen,
  and very pretty!

Who's this?	It's **Frank**.
What's **his** last name?	It's **Mann**.
How old is **he**?	**He's** twenty.
Is **he** tall or short?	**He's** short.
Is **he** chubby or thin?	**He's** thin.
What color is **his** hair?	It's **brown**.
What's **he** wearing?	**He's** wearing **a white shirt, a gray tie, a blue jacket, brown slacks and black shoes.**

Frank Mann

1. Joe Nunez   2. Susie Wong   3. Tim Grubb   4. Pat Pratt

PRONUNCIATION

I.   friend   next   yellow

      yes   twelve   dress

      red   ten   Ted

      sweater   bed   Fred

Fred is wearing a yellow sweater.

Ted's friend is twelve.

Fred is the boy in the red sweater.

II.   hat   lamp   bathrobe   Jack

      Sally   handsome   slacks   that

      black   Pat   jacket   last

      at   and   glasses   man

Jack is handsome.

That's my black hat.

Your glasses are under the lamp.

III.   My sweater is black.

Her red hat is on the bed.

My friend is wearing a yellow hat.

The black tie is on the bed.

He's wearing slacks, a bathrobe, and a sweater!

BASICS

STATEMENTS:
TO BE +
PREDICATE ADJECTIVE:

He is tall.   His hair is black.

She is chubby.   Her eyes are blue.

He is fifteen.   He's handsome.

INFORMATION QUESTIONS:

How old is he?   **Who's** that boy?

What's she like?   **Who's** this?

VOCABULARY/EXPRESSIONS

and	handsome	pretty
blond(e)	how old	short
boy	last (name)	tall
boyfriend	look	that
chubby	look at	there
eyes	man	thin
girl	new	very
girl friend	over there	woman
hair	pants	

numbers thirteen - twenty

TEST YOURSELF

I. Fill in with *in, on, at* or *under*.

1. Where is the sofa?   It's . . . the living room.

2. Where is the bed?   It's . . . the bedroom.

3. Where is the raincoat?   It's . . . the chair.

4. Where are the glasses?   They're . . . the table.

5. Where are the shoes?   They're . . . the floor.

6. Where's Don?
   a) It's three o'clock.
   b) At the bus stop.
   c) At six o'clock.

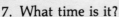

7. What time is it?
   a) It's quarter to six.
   b) At the bus stop.
   c) At six o'clock.

8. When is the next bus?
   a) It's three o'clock.
   b) At the bus stop.
   c) At half past six.

9. Who's Mary?
   a) Her hair is blonde.
   b) She is pretty.
   c) She is the girl in the red dress.

10. a) Who's Mary?
    b) What's Mary?
    c) Where's Mary?

She is behind Mr. Shale.

II.

1. Who's this? . . . .
2. How old is he? . . . .
3. What color is his hair? . . . .
4. Is he chubby or thin? . . . .
5. What color are his eyes? . . . .

Bill

6. . . . . ? It's Ann.
7. . . . . ? It's Taylor.
8. . . . . ? She's fifteen.
9. . . . . ? They're brown.
10. . . . . ? It's red.
11. . . . . ? She's tall.

III.

Mr. Price   Mr. Taylor   Mr. King   Mr. Novak

1. Where's Mr. Novak?   He's . . . . Mr. King.
2. Where's Mr. Taylor?   He's . . . . Mr. King.
3. Where's Mr. Price?   He's . . . . Mr. Taylor.
4. Where's Mr. King?   He's . . . . Mr. Taylor.

UNIT 5 FIVE

—Hi, dear.
 What's Peter doing?
—He's drinking tea
 in the living room.

—What's Mary doing?
—She's buying eggs at the store.

—And the dog?
—He's eating your newspaper.

My newspaper!

Do you like apples?

Yes.

No.

1. Do you like carrots?

2. Do you like nuts?

3. Do you like grapes?

4. Do you like pears?

5. Do you like candy bars?

6. Do you like beans?

7. Do you like oranges?

8. Do you like peaches?

9. Do you like sandwiches?

What's she buying? — She's buying eggs.

What's she buying? — She's buying carrots.

What's she buying? — She's buying pears.

What's she buying now?

1.
2.
3.
4.
5.
6.
7.
8.
9.

What's he eating?

1. He's eating a pear.

2. He's eating a banana.

3. He's eating a candy bar.

4. He's eating an apple.

5. He's eating an egg.

6. He's eating an orange.

What's he eating now?

1.

2.

3.

4.

5.

6.

She's buying a banana.

She's buying an apple.

She's buying eggs.

What's she buying?

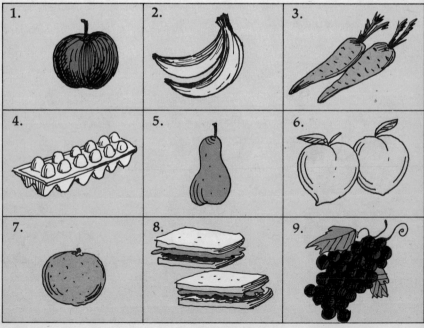

What's he drinking?  He's drinking coffee.

1. What's she drinking? She's drinking water.

2. What's she drinking? She's drinking lemonade.

3. What's he drinking?  He's drinking tea.

What's she eating? She's eating bread.

1. What's he eating?  He's eating ice cream.

2. What's he eating?  He's eating meat.

3. What's she eating?  She's eating cheese.

1. What's he doing?  He's drinking.

   What's he drinking? He's drinking milk.

2. What's she doing?  She's eating.

   What's she eating? She's eating fish.

What's s(he) doing?

1.

2.

3.

4.

IN THE STORE

Dick is in the store.
Carol is in the store.
Mrs. Hill is in the store.
She is the owner.

MRS. HILL: Hello, Dick.

DICK: Hello, Mrs. Hill.

This is my friend, Carol.

MRS. HILL: Hello, Carol.

Pleased to meet you.

CAROL: Hello, Mrs. Hill.

Nice to meet *you.*

MRS. HILL: Can I help you?

DICK: Eight candy bars, please.

MRS. HILL: Here you are.

Anything else?

CAROL: Yes, six

sandwiches, please.

MRS. HILL: Is that all?

DICK: Yes, thanks,

How much is that?

MRS. HILL: That's four dollars, please.

CAROL: Here you are.

Thank you.

Where's he sitting? He's sitting
on a chair.

Where's she sitting? She's sitting
in an armchair.

1. on a stool

2. in a bathtub

3. in a car

4. on a sofa

What's he doing? He's sitting
in an armchair.

1.

2.

3.

4.

What's she reading?		She's reading a book.

1. **a letter**   2. **a comic book**   3. **a newspaper**

Dick is in his room.
He's sitting on the bed.
He's eating an apple.
He's drinking milk.
He's reading a book.

Mary is in her room.
She's sitting on the rug.
She's eating a pear.
She's drinking lemonade.
She's reading a comic book.

And Don?

And Carol?

THE PRESENT PROGRESSIVE:

What is he doing?

	is buying	a banana.
	is eating	bread.
He	is drinking	coffee.
	is reading	a book.
	is sitting	in an armchair.

USE OF ARTICLES:

He's eating **a** pear.   He's eating pears.

He's eating **an** apple.   He's eating apples.

He's eating fish.   He's drinking tea.

PLURAL OF NOUNS:

one carrot   three carrots

one egg   four eggs

one peach   five peaches

VOCABULARY/EXPRESSIONS

an
apple(s)
armchair
banana(s)
bathtub
beans
book
bread
buying
candy bar(s)
car
carrot(s)
cheese
coffee
comic book
do

dog
doing
dollars
drinking
eating
egg(s)
fifty
fish
forty
grapes
ice cream
lemonade
letter
like
meat
milk

newspaper
nuts
orange(s)
owner
peaches
pear(s)
please
reading
sandwich(es)
sitting
stool
store
tea
water

Anything else?
Can I help you?
Here you are.
Hi, dear.
How much is that?
Is that all?
Nice to meet you.
Thank you.
Thanks.

—Tom! Hello, how *are* you?
—Fine, Rita. How are *you*?
—Not bad. Are you still a student?
—No, I'm a teacher now. How about you?
—I'm a doctor now.

—Are you still **a secretary?**

—No, I'm **an executive** now.

1. flight attendant   pilot

2. nurse   doctor

3. taxi driver   lawyer

4. engineer   architect

5. accountant   army officer

6. waiter   chef

1. I'm Eduardo Jimenez. I'm Colombian. I'm twenty. I'm a football player.

2. I'm Rita Perez. I'm Mexican. I'm twenty-seven. I'm a nurse.

3. I'm Susie Wong. I'm American. I'm nineteen. I'm a student.

4. I'm Maria Muniz. I'm Brazilian. I'm twenty-five. I'm a teacher.

5. I'm Pierre Goulet. I'm Canadian. I'm twenty-four. I'm a pilot.

6. I'm Tomás Moreno. I'm Puerto Rican. I'm thirty-eight. I'm a doctor.

NAME	NATIONALITY	AGE	OCCUPATION
1. Eduardo Jimenez	Colombia	20	
2. Rita Perez	Mexican	27	
3. Susie Wong	American	19	
4. Maria Muniz	Brazilian	25	
5. Pierre Goulet	Canadian	24	
6. Tomás Moreno	PR	38	
7. (for *you*)		8	

1. Are you Colombian?   No, I'm not.
   Are you Mexican?   No, I'm not.
   Are you American?   Yes, I am.

2. Are you twenty-six?   No, I'm not.
   Are you nineteen?   Yes, I am.

3. Are you a taxi driver?   No, I'm not.
   Are you a student?   Yes, I am.

4. You're Nancy Novak!   That's right.

Mexican 28 accountant Juan Fernandez	American 26 chef Nak Choung	Colombian 24 nurse Gloria Caldo
Brazilian 27 doctor Dr. Blume	Colombian 24 teacher Philippo Testa	Mexican 28 secretary Marta Sanchez
American 19 taxi driver Mario Martini	Brazilian 27 army officer General Branco	Mexican 19 flight attendant Margarita Gonzalez
Colombian 20 architect Elena Silva	American 19 student Nancy Novak	Brazilian 20 waiter Reynaldo Castro

PASSPORT CONTROL

—Good morning.
—Good morning. What's your name, please?
—My name is **Pat Goldman.**
—Are you **American?**
—Yes, I am.
—How old are you?
—I'm **twenty-six.**
—And what's your **occupation?**
—I'm **a doctor.**
—How long are you staying?
—Two weeks.
—Thank you. That's all.
—Thank *you*. Good-bye.

NAME	NATIONALITY	AGE	OCCUPATION
1. Pat Goldman	American	26	doctor
2. Roberto Flores	Mexican	33	teacher
3. John Cooper	English	19	secretary
4. Maria Tiant	Puerto Rican	29	pilot
5. Miguel Pinto	Venezuelan	30	executive
6. Aki Hiroshi	Japanese	22	accountant

LISTEN & UNDERSTAND

PRONUNCIATION

I. nuts   socks   skirts

     boots   hats   slacks

     grapes   books   shorts

What's Mary eating?

Nuts and carrots.

II. candy bars   jeans   beans

     eggs   pears   shoes

     chairs   girls   beds

He's eating eggs.

She's wearing red shoes.

III. oranges   peaches   sandwiches

     blouses   buses   glasses

That girl is buying two new blouses.

I'm eating peaches and oranges.

IV. Who's this?

Sue's buying oranges, pears, nuts and apples.

She's wearing red socks and white shoes.

BASICS

STATEMENTS

TO BE + PREDICATE
NOUN/ADJECTIVE:

I am Elena Silva.

You are pretty.

He is an accountant.

She is nineteen.

He is Mexican.

PRONOUNS YOU & I:

Are you Colombian?

Yes, I am.   No, I'm not.

VOCABULARY/EXPRESSIONS

accountant	nationality
age	nurse
am	occupation
architect	pilot
army officer	secretary
chef	sixty
doctor	staying
engineer	still
executive	student
flight attendant	taxi driver
football player	teacher
for	waiter
how long . . . ?	weeks
lawyer	

Fine.	Not bad.
How are you?	That's all.
How about you?	That's right.

TEST YOURSELF

I.

1. Hello Jerry. How are you?
   a) I'm fine, thanks.
   b) No, I'm not, thanks.
   c) I'm eighteen, thanks.

2. How old are you?
   a) Yes, I am.
   b) I'm seventeen.
   c) No, I'm a student now.

3. What's Ann doing? She's
   a) doing
   b) drinking tea.
   c) eating

4. What's Janet doing? She's
   a) sitting
   b) eating meat.
   c) doing

5. What's Pat doing? She's
   a) drinking
   b) reading a letter.
   c) doing

6. What's Sally doing? She's
   a) sitting
   b) doing in the car.
   c) buying

7. Here you are. Anything else?
   a) No, I'm not, thank you.
   b) That's all, thank you.
   c) Very well, thank you.

II. What's she buying? She's buying:

a) apples
b) sandwiches
c) eggs
d) pears
e) candy bars
f) carrots
g) nuts
h) oranges
i) ice cream
j) peaches
k) grapes
l) bread
m) fish
n) meat
o) cheese

III. Fill in with *a* or *an* where needed.

1. What's she buying?   She's buying... eggs.
2. What's he drinking?   He's drinking... water.
3. What's she eating?   She's eating... banana.
4. What's he eating?   He's eating... apple.
5. What's his occupation?   He's... accountant.
6. What's her occupation?   She's... pilot.

IV.

Puerto Rican 32 pilot John	American 22 accountant Betty
Mexican 23 nurse Carmen	Canadian 26 doctor Tom

1. Is .... still a nurse?   Yes, she is.
2. What's her nationality?   She's ....
3. Is Tom a ....?   Yes, he is.
4. What's ....?   He's Canadian.
5. ....?   He's twenty-six.
6. Is Betty still an ....?   Yes, she is.
7. Is John still a chef?   No, he isn't. He's a ......now.
8. ....?   He's Puerto Rican.

UNIT 7
SEVEN

—This is my family in 1918.
—Who's this?
—It's my grandmother.

THE JOHNSON FAMILY

The Parents

Patricia Johnson (Pat)
mother
wife
48

Thomas Johnson (Tom)
father
husband
45

The Children

Thomas Johnson, Jr. (Tommy)
son
brother
15

Susan Johnson (Susie)
daughter
sister
21

I'm Pat Johnson. I'm a housewife. My husband's name is Tom. He's a chef. I'm forty-eight years old. Tom is forty-five. Tommy is my son. He's fifteen. Susie is my daughter. She's twenty-one. Tommy is still a student. Susie is an accountant.

1. Who is Tommy's father?	Thomas Johnson is.
2. Who is Tommy's sister?	Susie is.
3. Who is Tom's wife?	Patricia Johnson is.
4. Who is Pat Johnson's son?	Tommy is.
5. Who is a housewife?	Pat is.
6. Who is a chef?	Tom is.
7. Who are the Johnson children?	Tommy and Susie are.
8. Who are Susie's parents?	Patricia and Thomas Johnson are.

1. —Are you eighteen?
   —No, I'm not.
   —Are you nineteen?
   —Yes, I am.

2. —Are you mother and
      daughter?
   —No, we're not.
   —Are you grandmother and
      granddaughter?
   —Yes, we are.

3. —Are you husband and
      wife?
   —No, we're not.
   —Are you brother and
      sister?
   —No, we're not.
   —Well, are you father and
      daughter?
   —Yes, we are.

4. —Are they brother and
      sister?
   —No, they're not.
   —Are they husband and
      wife?
   —No, they're not.
   —Are they mother and son?
   —Yes, they are.

5. —Are you father and son?
   —No, we're not.
   —Are you brothers?
   —No, we're not.
   —Are you friends?
   —Yes, we are.
      We're good friends.

6. —Are you the grandfather?
   —No, I'm not.
   —Are you the father?
   —No, I'm not.
   —Well, what *are* you?
   —I'm the grandson!

I'm handsome.  We're handsome!
Joe is handsome, too. We are both handsome.

1. Betty is happy. I'm happy, too.
2. I'm tired. My sister is tired, too.
3. I'm twenty-one. Rita is twenty-one, too.
4. Lucy is funny. I'm funny, too.
5. I'm cold. Daniel is cold, too.
6. Don is thin. I'm thin, too.

You're handsome,   You're handsome!
and so is your friend. You are both handsome.

1. You are beautiful, and so is your friend.
2. You are friendly, and so is your sister.
3. Your friend is angry, and so are you.
4. Susan is short, and so are you.
5. You are pretty, and so is your friend.
6. She is tall, and so are you.

Which **coat** is **Jack's**? The **big** coat is.

1. scarf/Maria's old

2. dog/Mike's friendly

3. hat/Betty's new

4. baby/Gloria's chubby

1. Is Tom in the car?

No, he's not.
He's *under* the car!

2. Is the cat on
   the bed?

No, it's not.
It's on the *table!*

3. Are the children
   in the yard?

No, they're not.
They're in the *bathtub!*

4. Is Peter in front of
   the chair?

No, he's not.
He's *behind* the chair!

5. Is the girl under
   the sofa?

No, she's not.
She's *on* the sofa!

6. Are you in the car?

No, I'm not.
I'm in the *bedroom!*

7. Are you under
   the table?

No, we're not.
We're *on* the table!

8. Is your grandmother
   behind the armchair?

No, she's not.
She's *in* the armchair!

1. Which room is she in?
   Is she in the kitchen?
   What's she doing?

   Yes, she is.
   She's cooking.

2. Which room is he in?
   Is he in the bathroom?
   What's he doing?

   Yes, he is.
   He's reading a book.

3. Which room are you in?
   Are you in the living room?
   Where *are* you?
   What are you doing?

   No, I'm not.
   I'm in the bedroom.
   I'm watching TV.

4. Which room is she in?
   Is she in the kitchen?
   Where *is* she?
   What's she doing?

   No, she's not.
   She's in the living room.
   She's listening to record

5. Are they in the bedroom?
   Where *are* they?
   What are they doing?

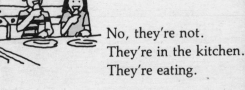

   No, they're not.
   They're in the kitchen.
   They're eating.

The Johnson family is at home. Mr. Johnson is in the kitchen. He is cooking. Mrs. Johnson is in the living room. She is sitting in an armchair. She's reading a newspaper. Tommy and his friend, Ricky, are in the yard. They are washing the car. Susie and her friend, Carol, are in Susie's bedroom. They are listening to records.

1.	Is Mr. Johnson in the living room?	No, he isn't. He's in the kitchen.
2.	Is Mrs. Johnson in the kitchen?	No, she isn't. She's in the living room
3.	Is Mrs. Johnson reading a book?	No, she isn't. She's reading a newspaper.
4.	Are Tommy and Ricky in the kitchen?	No, they aren't. They're in the yard.
5.	Are they washing the bus?	No, they aren't. They're washing the car.
6.	Are Susie and Carol in the kitchen?	No, they aren't. They're in Susie's bedroom.

LISTEN & UNDERSTAND

1. Mr. Gianetto is
   a) in the kitchen.
   b) in the living room.
   c) in the bathroom.

2. Mr. Gianetto is
   a) reading.
   b) listening to records.
   c) cooking.

3. Mrs. Gianetto is
   a) in the bedroom.
   b) in the kitchen.
   c) in the living room.

4. Mrs. Gianetto is
   a) reading.
   b) washing.
   c) cooking.

5. The boys are
   a) in the yard.
   b) in the kitchen.
   c) in the living room.

6. The boys are washing
   a) the dog.
   b) the car.
   c) the cat.

7. Susan is
   a) in her bedroom.
   b) in the bathroom.
   c) in the kitchen.

8. Susan is
   a) reading.
   b) eating.
   c) drinking.

9. The cat is
   a) under a chair in the living room.
   b) under a chair in the kitchen.
   c) on a chair in the living room.

INFORMATION QUESTIONS:

Who is Tommy's father?

Which coat is Jack's?

PERSONAL PRONOUNS:

I	am	eighteen.
He		chubby.
She	is	handsome.
It		at home.
We		
You	are	friends.
They		

POSSESSIVE OF NOUNS:

's

Tommy is Susie's brother.

Mr. and Mrs. Johnson are Tommy's parents.

NEGATIVE CONTRACTIONS:

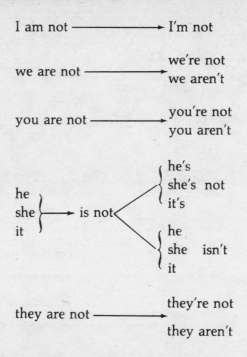

I am not ⟶ I'm not

we are not ⟶ we're not / we aren't

you are not ⟶ you're not / you aren't

he / she / it → is not ⟨ he's / she's / it's not; he / she / it isn't ⟩

they are not ⟶ they're not / they aren't

VOCABULARY/EXPRESSIONS

angry	friendly	so
baby	funny	son
bathroom	granddaughter	tired
beautiful	grandfather	too
big	grandmother	TV
both	happy	washing
brother(s)	housewife	watching
cat	husband	we
children	kitchen	which
coat	listening to	wife
cold	mother	wrong
cooking	parents	yard
daughter	records	years (old)
family	seventy	at home
father	sister	

—Come on over, Gloria.
  All our friends are here.
—Is Joe there?
—Yes, he is. He's playing the guitar.
—Are Tom and Betty there?
—Yes, they are. They're dancing.
—Is Nancy there?
—Yes, she is. She's singing.
—Is David there?
—Yes, he is. He's waiting for you!

Where's Peter going?  He's going to the bank.

1. Where's she going?  She's going to the post office.

2. Where are you going?  I'm going to the supermarket.

3. Where are you going?  We're going to the train station.

4. Where are they going?  They're going to the bus station.

5. Where are they going?  They're going to the
police station.

6. Where's it going?  It's going to the
airport.

7. Where's he going?  He's going to the
theater.

8. Where's she going?  She's going to the
library.

9. Where are they going?  They're going to the
garage.

What's he doing?  He's singing.

1. What's she doing?  She's driving.

2. What's he doing?  He's sleeping.

3. What are they doing? They're dancing.

4. What are they doing?  They're playing American football.

5. What are they doing?  They're watching TV.

—Hello.
—Hello, is this Tom?
—Yes, it is.
—Hi, Tom. This is Juan.
  How are you?
—Fine, how are *you?*
—Fine, thanks. What are you doing?
—Ben is here. We're **watching TV.**
  Come on over.

1. reading

2. listening to records

3. drinking coffee

4. playing the guitar

5. eating sandwiches

6. listening to the radio

How many tables are there?   There is one table.
How many lamps are there?   There are two lamps.

1. How many boys are there?   There are three boys.

2. How many guitars are there?   There are three guitars.

3. How many radios are there?   There is one radio.

4. How many lamps are there?   There are two lamps.

5. How many rugs are there?   There is one rug.

6. How many records are there?   There are four records.

7. How many chairs are there?   There are two chairs.

8. How many tables are there?   There is one table.

—Is there one **bank**,
  or are there two **banks** here?
—There are two **banks**.

1. **supermarket**

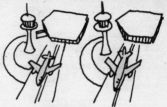

2. **airport**

3. **hotel**

4. **theater**

—Is there one **library**,
  or are there two **libraries** here?
—There are two **libraries**.

1. **cemetery (cemeteries)**

2. **baby (babies)**

3. **strawberry (strawberries)**

4. **country (countries)**

—Is there one **garage**,
  or are there two **garages** here?
—There are two **garages**.

1. church (churches)

2. sandwich (sandwiches)

2. bridge (bridges)

4. brush (brushes)

—Is there one **man**,
  or are there two **men** here?
—There are two **men**.

1. woman (women)

2. child (children)

3. foot (feet)

4. tooth (teeth)

—What are you doing?
—I'm **reading a book**.

1.

2.

3.

4.

5.

6.

7.

8.

9.

Greenfield is a small village in England. It's not far from Manchester. There are five buses to Manchester every day, but there is only one train. There aren't many people on the train at six o'clock in the morning.

The church is in the middle of the village on the square. There are many other buildings on the square. There is a bank, the post office, the bus station and the police station. The library is behind the police station.

There are two garages in front of the bridge. There is a small cemetery behind the church. It's a small village, isn't it? There is no traffic, no noise, and no pollution.

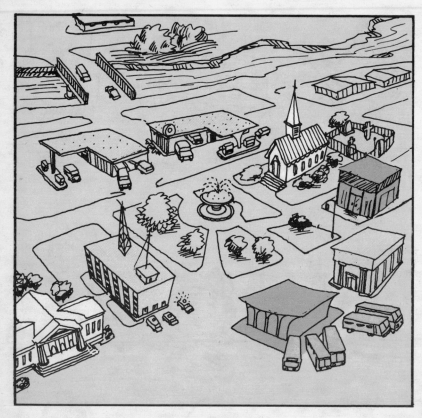

1. Where is Greenfield?
2. How many buses are there to Manchester?
3. Are there many people on the train?
4. What is in the middle of the village?
5. What other buildings are on the square?
6. Where's the library?
7. What are there in front of the bridge?
8. What's behind the church?

Boston is a small city, but there are many squares in it. This is Copley Square. The big Boston Public Library is on one side. There is an old church across from the library. There is a bus stop in front of the library.

There is a tall office building behind the library. You can see all of Boston from there. There are other buildings around the square. Some are old; some are new. It's a pretty square, isn't it? But there is a lot of traffic and a lot of noise in Boston. There is pollution, too.

1. Now ask and answer questions about Boston and Copley Square.

2. What about *your* city? What's it like?

LISTEN & UNDERSTAND

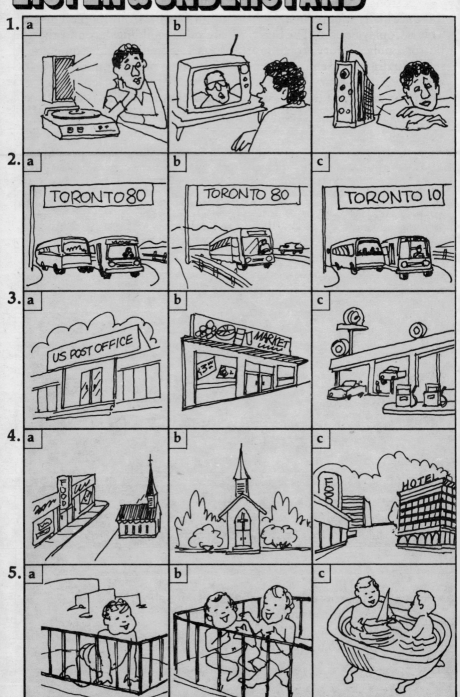

PRONUNCIATION

I. she   tea   see
    green   cheese   eating
    meat   please   peach
    Peter   teacher   three

    She's reading.
    Peter's eating a green peach.

II. six   fish   sitting
    milk   drinking   in
    it   is   Bill
    still   English   Tim

    Is Bill drinking milk?
    Tim is sitting in the living room.

III. banks   guitars   blouses
     airports   records   brushes
     hats   schools   watches
     weeks   hotels   offices
     bus   trees   churches
     across   flowers   bridges

BASICS

INFORMATION QUESTIONS:

Where's he going?

How many lamps are there?

STATEMENTS:

There is one train station.

There are two bus stations.

NOUN PLURALS:

bank	bus	country	church
banks	buses	countries	churches
child	foot	man	woman
children	feet	men	women

VOCABULARY/EXPRESSIONS

across from	feet	radio(s)
airport(s)	foot	side
a lot of	from	singing
all	garage(s)	sleeping
around	going	small
babies	guitar(s)	some
bank(s)	here	square(s)
bridge(s)	hotel(s)	strawberry(ies)
brush(es)	how many	supermarket(s)
buildings	in the middle of	teeth
bus station(s)	library(ies)	theater(s)
but	men	to
cemetery(ies)	noise	tooth
child	of	traffic
church(es)	office	train
city	only	train station
country(ies)	other	village
dancing	our	waiting for
day	people	women
driving	playing	
eighty	police station	Come on over.
every	pollution	
far	post office	

TEST YOURSELF

I. Fill in with *is*, *am*, or *are*.

1. They ... pretty.　　　　2. I ... a student.

3. You ... handsome.　　　4. The apples ... on the table.

5. **a)** He
   b) I　　　is in the kitchen.
   c) They

6. **a)** She
   b) I　　　are children.
   c) They

II.

Mr. Riley　　　Mrs. Riley　　　Conor Riley　　　Anne Riley
(Paul)　　　　(Judy)

1. Who is Judy's　　**a)** son?
　　　　　　　　　b) daughter?　　Conor is.
　　　　　　　　　c) wife?

2. Who is Paul's　　**a)** son?
　　　　　　　　　b) daughter?　　Anne is.
　　　　　　　　　c) wife?

3. Who is Paul's　　**a)** mother?
　　　　　　　　　b) wife?　　　　Judy is.
　　　　　　　　　c) husband?

4. Who is Conor's　**a)** sister?
　　　　　　　　　b) brother?　　Anne is.
　　　　　　　　　c) family?

5. Who are Conor's　**a)** parents?
　　　　　　　　　b) children?　　Paul and Judy are.
　　　　　　　　　c) friends?

III. How many are there?

Begin your answers with *there is* or *there are*.

1.

2.

3.

4.

5.

6.

7.

8.

IV.

1. What's John doing?   He's
   a) eating.
   b) playing the guitar.
   c) sleeping.

2. What's Mary doing?   She's
   a) drinking.
   b) listening to records.
   c) singing.

3. What's Sam doing?   He's
   a) eating.
   b) singing.
   c) sleeping.

4. What's Helen doing?   She's
   a) washing.
   b) sleeping.
   c) dancing.

V. 1. What . . . .?   They're watching TV.

2. Where . . . .?   We're going to the library.

3. How . . . . .there?   There are two babies.

4. Is there one man, or   There are two . . . .
   are there . . . . here?

5. Is there one woman there?   No, there are two . . . .

6. Is there one library in Millville?   No, there are four . . . .

7. My friend is tall and so are you.   Yes, ...

8. Your brother is handsome, and   Yes, ...
   . . . . I.

VI. 1. Where's the bus going?   . . . .

2. Where's Frank going?   . . . .

3. Where's Beth going?   . . . .

4. Where's Henry going?   . . . .

VII. 1. Am I handsome?   No, ...

2. Are you twenty?   No, ...

3. Is Alice twenty?   No, ...

4. Are they brother and sister?   No, ...

—Whose cup is this?
—It's Mary's.
—Well, give it to her.

—Whose glasses are these?
—They're Juan's.
—Well, give them to him.

1. *This* racket is old, but *that* racket is new.

2. *This* is a Canadian player, and *that* is a Mexican player.

3. *These* roller skates are Peter's, and *those* ice skates are Mary's.

4. *These* circles are big, but *those* squares are small.

1. This is an English student.   These are Japanese students.

2. That is a Turkish pilot.   Those are Colombian pilots.

3. These are American footballs.   Those are Brazilian footballs.

What are they saying? Use **this**, **that**, **these** or **those** in your answers.

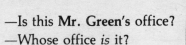

—Is this **Mr. Green's** office?   —No, it isn't.
—Whose office *is* it? —It's **Ms. Pott's.**

—Is this your **shirt**? —No, it isn't.
—Whose **shirt** *is* it? —It's **Tom Marks's.**

1. sweater/Mike Jones's   4. car/Maria March's

2. hat/Betty Church's   5. boyfriend/Sally Burns's

3. tie/Dennis's   6. racket/James's

—Is this your **rug**? —No, it isn't.
—Whose **rug** *is* it? —It's **the Greens'.**

1. bedroom/the boys'   4. football/the students'

2. teacher/the girls'   5. store/the Johnsons'

3. car/the Blacks'   6. garage/the Kings'

THE COSTUME PARTY

What's Dick wearing?

1. Bess's hat

2. . . . .

3. . . . .

4. Mary's blouse

5. Bess's skirt

6. Fred's pants

7. . . . .

8. Betty's shoes

What's Mike wearing?

1. . . . .

2. . . . .

3. . . . .

4. . . . .

5. . . . .

6. . . . .

7. . . . .

8. . . . .

I	am			me.
He	is			him.
She				her.
		tired, so Jack's helping		
We				us.
You	are			you.
They				them.

	my		me.
	his		him.
That's	her	book, so give it to	her.
	our		us.
	their		them.

—Whose **pen** is this?
—It's **Tom's.**
—Well, give it to **him.**

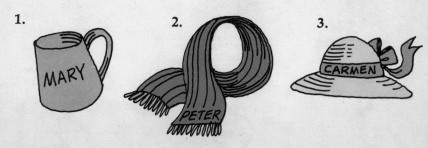

1.

2.

3.

Who's this?
It's Tom.

What's this?
It's a book.
Whose is it?
It's Tom's.

What's Tom doing?
He's reading.

1. Mary

2. James

3. Lucy

4. Mr. Dodds

5. Bess

LISTEN & UNDERSTAND

BASICS

POSSESSIVE OF NOUNS:

Whose shirt is this? It's the Browns'.
the boys'.
Jack's.
Bess's.

OBJECT PRONOUNS:

Give the book to **me**. Tom is helping me.
you.
him.
her.
us.
them.

DEMONSTRATIVE ADJECTIVES/PRONOUNS:

 **this** car

 that car

these cars
These are cars.

those cars
Those are cars.

POSSESSIVE ADJECTIVES:
Our
Your dog is very big.
Their

VOCABULARY/EXPRESSIONS

circles	ice skates	their
costume party	me	them
cup	ninety	these
give	office	those
gloves	pen	us
helping	racket	whose
her	roller skates	
him	so	

1. What time is it?   It's ten-fifteen.

2. What time is it?   It's ten-thirty.

3. What time is it?   It's ten-twenty.

4. What time is it?   It's ten forty-five.

—Hurry, it's late.
—What time is it?
—It's **ten-twenty.**
—No, it isn't. It's only **nine-thirty.** It's early.

1.   2.

3.   4.

1. When are you going? In the morning.

2. When are you going? In the evening.

3. When are you going? In the afternoon.

4. When are you going? At noon.

5. When are you going? At midnight.

6. When are you going? At night.

—Good afternoon.
—Good afternoon, sir.
—When is your next flight to Mexico?
—Tomorrow at **seven**.
—Seven **in the morning**, or seven **in the evening**?
—**In the evening**. It's flight 602.
—Thank you.
—Thank you, sir. Good-bye.

1.	9:00	**morning/night**
2.	12:00	**noon/midnight**
3.	5:00	**morning/afternoon**

—Where are you going?
—I'm going to **London.**
—Who's going with you?
—**My mother** is.
—When are you going?
—**At ten o'clock.**

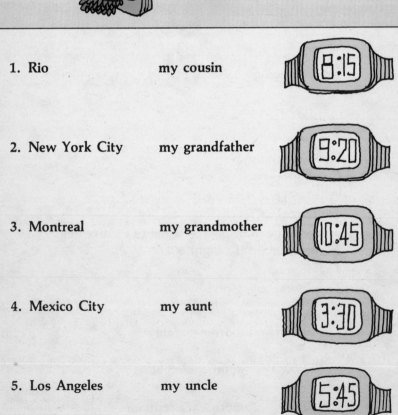

1. Rio   my cousin   8:15

2. New York City   my grandfather   9:20

3. Montreal   my grandmother   10:45

4. Mexico City   my aunt   3:30

5. Los Angeles   my uncle   5:45

—What are you doing **tonight**?
—I'm going to **a party**.
—What are you wearing?
—I'm wearing my **new blouse**,
  my **red skirt**, and
  my **black boots**.
—When are you going?
—**At seven-thirty**.

1. tonight
   a dance
   blue dress, yellow scarf
   8:00

2. today
   the movies
   old jeans, white sweater
   4:30

3. this morning
   church
   brown coat, red hat
   6:30

4. this afternoon
   the football game
   yellow suit, brown shoes
   2:15

5. tomorrow night
   a concert
   black dress, white coat
   7:30

6. Saturday night
   the museum
   new slacks, gray blouse,
   green jacket
   8:15

LISTEN & UNDERSTAND

PRONUNCIATION

I.
tall	teacher	ten	suit
to	eight	tonight	meat
cemetery	water	stop	pilot

Our teacher is tall.

We're going tonight at ten to eight.

II.
building	side	around	bedroom
dancing	daughter	drinking	old
dress	child	lemonade	blonde

Her daughter is drinking lemonade.

Don is very handsome.

III.
thin	theater	three
thirty	both	thanks

Bill and Sam are both thin.

We're going to the theater at three-thirty.

IV.
that	these	other
father	there	brother
mother	they	them

That's my brother over there.

My mother's father is my grandfather.

V. That's Tom's lemonade.

My father is a teacher.

Tom's going to the theater with his brother tonight.

They are both drinking tea.

They're going to London at two-thirty.

BASICS

TIME PHRASES:

I'm going

- in the afternoon.
- in the morning.
- in the evening.
- today.
- tonight.
- tomorrow.
- now.
- at midnight.
- at noon.
- at night.
- this morning
- this afternoon

TIME STRUCTURES:

It's ten-twenty (10:20).

It's ten-thirty (10:30).

QUESTION WORDS:

Where are you going?	**To London.**
When are you going?	**At ten o'clock in the morning.**
Who's going with you?	**John is.**

VOCABULARY/EXPRESSIONS

afternoon	museum	Good afternoon.
aunt	night	Hurry!
concert	one hundred	It's late (early).
cousin	sir	
dance	today	
evening	tomorrow	
flight	tonight	
football game	uncle	
movies	with	

TEST YOURSELF

I.

1. I'm tired, so Frank's helping
   - a) them.
   - b) me.
   - c) us.

2. We're tired, so Frank's helping
   - a) us.
   - b) me.
   - c) you.

3. They're tired, so Frank's helping
   - a) her.
   - b) them.
   - c) him.

4. That's
   - a) their
   - b) our
   - c) her

   book, so give it to them.

5. This is
   - a) his
   - b) her
   - c) your

   scarf. Give it to him.

II. Fill in with *this*, *that*, *these* or *those*.

1. Look at . . . skates over there.

2. Is . . . your mother across the street?

3. Who are . . . players over there?

4. Aren't . . . shoes in that store pretty?

5. Here you are. . . . is your ice cream.

6. . . . grapes on that table are good, too.

7. Are . . . glasses here Tom's?

8. . . . are my boots; . . . are your boots under the table.

III.

1. .... hat is that?   It's John's.

2. .... shoes are these?   .... Sally's.

3. These books are Mike Jones's.   Well, give ....

4. This is your pen.   Well, give ....

5. ....?   I'm going to London.

6. .... to London?   Tomorrow.

7. .... going with your sister?   No, I'm not.

8. ....?   My brother is.

9. What time is it?   It's ....

10. What time is it?   It's ....

11. What time is it? 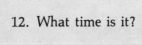   It's ....

12. What time is it?   It's ....

—Can you type?
—No, I can't.

—Can you take shorthand?
—No, I can't.

—Can you make coffee?
—Yes, I can.
—Good. You're hired.

Can Sally skate?  **No, she can't.**

1. Can Sam type?  No, he can't.

2. Can they ski?  Yes, they can.

3. Can they run?  Yes, they can.

4. Can it sing?  Yes, it can.

5. Can it sing?  No, it can't.

6. Can you walk?  No, we can't.

7. Can he drive?  No, he can't.

Can you help me? No, I'm sorry. I have to wash the clothes.

1. Can Tommy help me?  No, I'm sorry. He has to study.

2. Can Susan help me?  No, I'm sorry. She has to clean the windows.

3. Can Bill help me?  No, I'm sorry. He has to brush the dog.

4. Can Fred and Ron help me?  No, I'm sorry. They have to polish the car.

5. Well, I'm going to play tennis.  No, you can't. You have to help *me!*

—Mom, can I go to the **movies?**
—No, you can't. You have to do your homework.

1. tennis match **2. concert** **3. museum** **4. theater**

—Can you **skate?**
—No, I can't.

1.

2.

3.

4.

1. What sport can he play?

He can play soccer.

2. What sport can she play?

She can play baseball.

3. What sport can they play?

They can play tennis.

4. What sport can you play?

I can play table tennis.

—What game can he play?
—He can play **chess**.

1. backgammon

2. cards

3. checkers

4. Monopoly

1. What instrument can she play? She can play the bass.

2. What instrument can he play?  He can play the drums.

3. What instrument can they play?  They can play the piano

4. What instrument can you play? I can play the flute.

—Can he **play baseball?**
—Yes, he's **playing baseball** now.

1. skate 2. swim 3. play chess

4. type 5. play tennis 6. play the bass

How about you? What can **you** *do?*

THE CONCERT

Jack is waiting for Gloria.
They're going to a rock concert.
The concert is at seven o'clock.
It's quarter to seven now.
But Gloria is late.
She's still at home.
She's washing her hair.

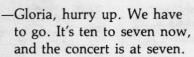

—Gloria, hurry up. We have
to go. It's ten to seven now,
and the concert is at seven.
—No, the concert is at eight.
Look in the newspaper.
—I *am* looking in the
newspaper. The concert is at
seven. Can't you read?
—Oh dear. I'm sorry. Well,
come in and wait.

—No, I can wait in the yard.
I can sit here and...
—No! Stop! You can't sit...
—Oh yes I can.
—Oh Jack. Look at your pants.
Look at your hands!
Look at the sign! Can't *you*
read?
—Oh. Wet Paint.
Well, don't hurry, Gloria.
I have to go home and
change my suit.

LISTEN & UNDERSTAND

BASICS

CAN:

I can swim. He can skate.
Can you make coffee?
Mom, can I go to the movies?

TO HAVE TO:

I		
You	have to	
They		go.
		study.
He		read this book.
She	has to	

VOCABULARY/EXPRESSIONS

backgammon	looking	swimming
baseball	make	table tennis
bass	Monopoly	tennis
cards	piano	tennis match
change	play	type
checkers	polish	typing
chess	read	wait
clean	rock concert	walk
clothes	run	wash
drive	sign	windows
drums	sing	
flute	sit	Come in.
game	skate	Good.
go	skating	Hurry up!
going to	ski	Oh dear.
hands	soccer	Stop!
hired	sport	take shorthand
homework	study	wet paint
instrument	swim	

UNIT 12 TWELVE

—Hello, James. How are you?
—Terrible!
—What's the matter with you?
—I have a bad **tooth.**

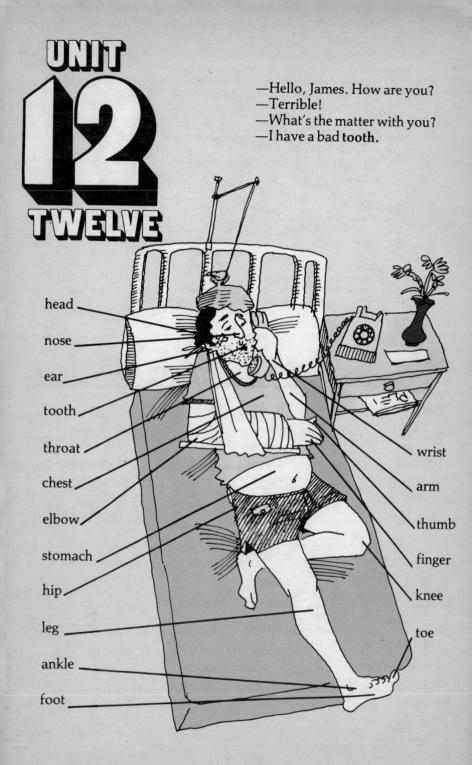

head
nose
ear
tooth
throat
chest
elbow
stomach
hip
leg
ankle
foot

wrist
arm
thumb
finger
knee
toe

—When are the **Smiths** coming for **dinner**?
—On **Sunday**.

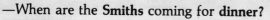

1.
2.
3.

4.
5.
6.

—When are you taking your vacation this year?
—In **January**.
—Oh, do you like a **winter** vacation?
—Yes.

	January						
WINTER	S	M	T	W	T	F	S
		1	2	3	4	5	6
	7	8	9	10	11	12	13
	14	15	16	17	18	19	20
	21	22	23	24	25	26	27
	28	29	30	31			

	February						
WINTER	S	M	T	W	T	F	S
					1	2	3
	4	5	6	7	8	9	10
	11	12	13	14	15	16	17
	18	19	20	21	22	23	24
	25	26	27	28			

	March						
SPRING	S	M	T	W	T	F	S
					1	2	3
	4	5	6	7	8	9	10
	11	12	13	14	15	16	17
	18	19	20	21	22	23	24
	25	26	27	28	29	30	31

	April						
SPRING	S	M	T	W	T	F	S
	1	2	3	4	5	6	7
	8	9	10	11	12	13	14
	15	16	17	18	19	20	21
	22	23	24	25	26	27	28
	29	30					

	May						
SPRING	S	M	T	W	T	F	S
			1	2	3	4	5
	6	7	8	9	10	11	12
	13	14	15	16	17	18	19
	20	21	22	23	24	25	26
	27	28	29	30	31		

	June						
SUMMER	S	M	T	W	T	F	S
						1	2
	3	4	5	6	7	8	9
	10	11	12	13	14	15	16
	17	18	19	20	21	22	23
	24	25	26	27	28	29	30

	July						
SUMMER	S	M	T	W	T	F	S
	1	2	3	4	5	6	7
	8	9	10	11	12	13	14
	15	16	17	18	19	20	21
	22	23	24	25	26	27	28
	29	30	31				

	August						
SUMMER	S	M	T	W	T	F	S
				1	2	3	4
	5	6	7	8	9	10	11
	12	13	14	15	16	17	18
	19	20	21	22	23	24	25
	26	27	28	29	30	31	

	September						
FALL	S	M	T	W	T	F	S
							1
	2	3	4	5	6	7	8
	9	10	11	12	13	14	15
	16	17	18	19	20	21	22
	23	24	25	26	27	28	29
	30						

	October						
FALL	S	M	T	W	T	F	S
		1	2	3	4	5	6
	7	8	9	10	11	12	13
	14	15	16	17	18	19	20
	21	22	23	24	25	26	27
	28	29	30	31			

	November						
FALL	S	M	T	W	T	F	S
					1	2	3
	4	5	6	7	8	9	10
	11	12	13	14	15	16	17
	18	19	20	21	22	23	24
	25	26	27	28	29	30	

	December						
WINTER	S	M	T	W	T	F	S
							1
	2	3	4	5	6	7	8
	9	10	11	12	13	14	15
	16	17	18	19	20	21	22
	23	24	25	26	27	28	29
	30	31					

...eather like?   It's drizzling.

2. What's the weather like?   It's raining.

3. What's the weather like?   It's pouring.

4. What's the weather like?   It's snowing.

5. What's the weather like?   It's hot.

6. What's the weather like?   It's warm.

7. What's the weather like?   It's cold.

8. What's the weather like?   It's cloudy.

9. What's the weather like?   It's sunny.

10. What's the weather like?   It's windy.

—Hi, this is **John** in **San Francisco**.
—Hi, **John**.
 When are you coming?
—I'm leaving here at **nine o'clock**.
 What's the weather like there?
—It's hot and sunny here.
 What's the weather like in
 San Francisco?
—It's **raining**.
—Well, come and enjoy the sun.
—Right! See you soon.

—Hello, Tom. This is **Sue**.
—Hello, **Sue**. Where are you?
—I'm on vacation in **Florida**.
—What's the weather like?
—It's **hot**.

LISTEN & UNDERSTAND

BASICS

INFORMATION QUESTIONS:

> What's the matter with you?
> What's the weather like?
> When are they coming?

PREPOSITIONS OF TIME:

> They're coming **on** Friday.
> I'm going **in** December.
> I'm eating **at** eight.

PREDICATE ADJECTIVES:

> The weather is **sunny**.
> It's **warm**.

DAYS OF THE WEEK   MONTHS OF THE YEAR

VOCABULARY/EXPRESSIONS

after	head	thumb
ankle	hip	toe
arm	hot	vacation
bad	knee	warm
before	leaving	weather
breakfast	leg	windy
chest	lunch	winter
cloudy	nose	wrist
come	pouring	year
dinner	raining	
drinks	snowing	
drizzling	spring	See you soon.
ear	stomach	Terrible!
elbow	summer	What's the matter
enjoy	sun	with you?
fall	sunny	
finger	taking	
have	throat	

WORD LIST